Jesus

H e's

O ur

P ersonal

E vangelist

Jesus

H e's

O ur

P ersonal

E vangelist

_____

Gerald M. Allen

Jesus

H e's
O ur
P ersonal
E vangelist

Copyright © 2014 Gerald M. Allen
All rights reserved

Dedication

I wish to dedicate the poems in this book
to my loving wife, Ronnie, whom Father God
called home to be with Him.

Introduction

As a man of 74 years of age, and having been married to the love of my life for 52 1/2 years, my world was shaken when my love, Ronnie, was stricken with lung cancer in 2008. I remember the dreadful feeling of losing her after we had spent a lifetime together.

Through it all, she remained strong with her belief in our Lord and Savior Jesus Christ. When times were hard for me to understand not being able to help her, she would comfort me. She told me she knew she was in God's hands and was right where He wanted her to be.

Living all my life I believed there is a God and Jesus is His Son, but I had never been baptized. Ronnie made me promise to be baptized. Before she died we had a pastor come to the house and he baptized me.

I lost her on September 26, 2010.

Moving through the next couple years without my Ronnie, and not being a religious person, more and more I realized there was something missing from my life. Not just my Ronnie, but something much greater. Her faith in God our Father, God the Son, and God the Holy Spirit.

As the song goes, "count your blessings, name them one by one," I began to see there were some undesirable things in my early childhood, the Lord my God had brought me through.

God brought Ronnie and I together when I was 18 years old and she was 16 years old. We began our life together filled with Blessing after Blessing.

Were there some rough hard times? Absolutely! But there, once again, I now see how the Hand of God brought us through those tough times.

We were given four special blessings. Four loving daughters and through the love of God, my daughters brought forth eight more blessings. And thus far, one granddaughter, through God, has blessed me with a great-grandchild.

Though, I mention just a few of God's blessings on me, I know it would take a very large book with many many pages to list all the wondrous blessings God has placed upon me. The largest and best, His Son and my Savior Jesus Christ.

As I turned my face toward Jesus my life began to change. Through Jesus, my thoughts turned from myself to God and helping my fellow man.

As I moved along on my journey with Jesus, messages began to turn over and over in my mind. The feelings were overwhelming for me to write these messages down in poems.

It is my prayer that whoever reads these messaged poems will read them in the spirit that they were written. These poems could have been written by you, about you, and for you. Perhaps you will see moments and circumstances where the message might have come directly from your heart. I pray that if in some way you feel these messages are written with you in mind, that it lifts your eyes and heart to Father God.

I pray that any message you accept as fitting into your life will bring you closer to our Father God. In some way, you may be brought into a closer loving relationship with God. Through that, His great Loving Glory will fill you with unspeakable joy.

The Holy Spirit places the idea and then the words to be written in my hand to put forth a message.

I prayerfully hope that as you read these poems you will enjoy and accept any message that may touch your heart.

Remember: God's Blessings are always there in the love He has for you, and when things may get you down, hold out your hand, for the Father is there to take your hand and draw you to Him and the safety of His wonderful Love.

God Bless All and enjoy!

Gerald M. Allen

Welcome Home

When you're tired and you're weary
And you wonder where you're at
When your days are dark and dreary
And you can't help looking back.

To the days that are of sorrow
Of the sins and wrongs you did
And you worry of tomorrow
For you know that they're not hid.

There's a different way to do this
There's a path that leads to bliss
To a Man that walked among us
And He'll greet you with a kiss.

He took our sins upon Him
As they nailed Him to a cross
And through his blood and suffering
He died but was not lost.

For in the ground three days He lay
For all our sins to pay
The Lord our God then raised Him up
From the ground in which he lay.

So trust in Him, believe in Him
He'll lead you on your way
And through his blood and suffering
He will wash your sins away.

He will come to you and live in you
And guide you night and day
So praise our God who sent his Son
Our sins for Him to pay.

So never look behind you
But keep your eye ahead
For Christ our Lord, The King of Kings
Has Risen from the dead.

And on the day you kneel to Him
That sits upon His throne
He'll take your hand and lift you up
And tell you, Welcome Home.

Praise To Jesus

From the moment that I wake up
To the day that lies ahead
For my Holy God in Heaven
I do get me out of bed.

And the day that is before me
Let me walk it in God's way
For the path that God does show me
Is a place for me to pray.

As I raise my hands to reach to Him
And praise His Holy name
He holds me close and comforts me
That reaches deep within.

And when I sin
And sometimes go astray
He holds me up and strengthens me
And He loves me anyway.

Oh Lord my God do make of me
Of that which is Your will
To live my life with faithfulness
For His cross that's on that hill.

My heart my soul my spirit too
I gladly give to Him
He gave His life and spilled His blood
To wash away my sins.

And on the day I kneel to Him
Before His mighty throne
He'll take my hand and say to me
My child, you're welcome home.

A New Path

I was on a lonely path
There was darkness in my past
And I felt the darkness
Closing in on me.

Then I raised my hands above
And prayed God I need Your love
For I felt the time
Was running out on me.

But He wanted me to see
First things need there to be
Then a man of God
I went therefore to see.

Said the man of God to me
Of a thing that had to be
Then with the water and the word
He baptized me.

I confessed of all my sins
And sweet Jesus took them in
And He nailed them to
A cross on Calvary.

When Christ washed away my sins
Jesus took his place within
With a blinding love
That took a hold of me.

Now I'm on a Godly path
And there's brightness
Here at last, and I feel
His awesome love surrounding me.

Now I raise my hands above
And I thank Him for His love
And forever more
I'll Pray My God To Thee.

The Spirit

On the pillow lay my head
Of sweet dreams I had in bed
When the Holy Spirit
Did awaken me.

Hey you raise your weary head
And then get you out of bed
For there are some things
I want to say to Thee.

Let's go into the den
And there grab a pad and pen
And you better bring some
coffee on your way.

For if it takes all night
We're gonna get this right
So you write down
All the things I have to say.

Now He talked to me all night
Of the things for me to write
And He didn't stop
Until the break of day.

Now you wonder what he said?

Well some night when you're in bed
With your pillow tucked
Beneath your sleepy head.

And the Spirit He will come
Before your sleep is done
For at that time
He will awaken thee.

And He'll keep you up all night
Of the things for you to write
For there are some things
He'll want to say to thee.

For the words they won't be few
Of the things He'll say to you
So write down of all
He has to say.

To others you will say
How the Spirit had His way
And how He talked to you
All night till break of day.

Then with slightly bended ear
They'll lean close so they may hear
Then they'll look to you and ask

WELL WHAT'D HE SAY?

Reflections

When I look into the looking glass
And in there I do see
And I wonder of the image
That is looking back at me.

Is he truthful, is he faithful
Is there anything he's hid
Has he gave a full confession
Of all the things he did?

Does he do what God does ask of him
Does he do it right way
Does he try to live in righteousness
On each and every day?

In Christ His name, I pray for him
To wash away his sins
Yes, it is the answer
To the questions asked of him.

For the image in that looking glass
The image that I see
The image in the looking glass
That's the image there of me.

I pray someday in the looking glass
There the image I will see
Will be the image there of Jesus Christ
And the image not of me.

Old Mother Hubbard

Old Mother Hubbard
Went to her cupboard
But alas
Her poor cupboard was bare.

With a family to feed
How great was her need
For the food
That of which was not there.

Then from our Father above
Came His message of love
Through the Spirit
That all we do share.

Give heed to their need
And follow God's lead
For His Children
The burden they bare.

Then to all of God's glory
Make happy this story
And give all
Your best, plus a prayer.

God Bless

How Amazing All This Is

Just look yourself around you
On a very busy day
Of all that does surround you
Our God made for us one day.

The morning as the sun appears
So brightly there above
It's from the Lord our God
To show us all His love.

How bright there is the color
Of the clear blue skies above
It is God's glorious way
That starts our brand new day.

The green green grass
The flowers and the trees
And what a sweet aroma
That attracts the little bees.

God did bring forth great animals
How different they all be
But in them be a beauty
For all of us to see.

The vastness of the universe
Of all we cannot see

And of the stars at night
How countless they all be.

There is one special thing
Our Father set apart
The children in their laughter
That puts a smile within your heart.

So never take for granted
The things that God has done
As a sacrifice for all of us
He gave his only Son.

Christ our Lord did die for us
So that we may live
Don't close your eyes but look around
Of all that He does give

Now within your heart you know
You know
HOW AMAZING ALL THIS IS!

Empty Vessel Made of Clay

To the day that stands before me
As you guide me on my way
And your hand that does protect me
For Your plan that fits this day.

Without you Lord my Father
I'm a useless wretched man
But in you Lord my God
I always feel I can.

Your awesome great stability
You're ever still the same
Please give me Christ's humility
That I may glorify Your name.

Help me keep and love my neighbors
Give the poor a helping hand
Make me humble to all others
Make of me a useful man.

O Lord my God my Father
It's to You that I do pray
For Lord my God without You
I'm an empty vessel made of clay.

So take this empty vessel
That's only made of clay
And put there God within it
of Your will, and only of Your way.

Get Out Of That Ditch

Now you've driven down life's highway
And you run off in the ditch
So think of all the different ways
In your life that you can switch.

In your mind look deep within your heart
Feel the need there of the poor
Or is it there within your heart
To those you will ignore.

The need there for your fellow man
Is a need to not ignore
For when you help and see you can
You'll want to do much more.

The thought of yours for others
Fills the Spirit full of joy
From the Lord our God, through Jesus Christ
God's own begotten boy.

In Jesus Christ, devote your life
In the ditch you'll be no more
For all our sins Christ gave his life
And opened us a door.

As the Lord our God does change you
To the life that Jesus gives
Christ our Lord His life he give
And He did so we may live.

Now your back upon life's highway
Keep your eyes there straight ahead
Thank Christ our Lord and Savior
Whom our God raised from the dead.

So ask the Holy Spirit
How be the best that you can give
And praise our God in heaven
For He is the God that lives.

I Wonder

Sometimes I sit and wonder
Of Heaven which is my Father's home
He'll show to us His wonders
From there we'll never roam.

I'll be there with my wife again
Father called her home to be with Him
We'll remember years of married life
Fifty-two years, a gift to us from Him.

My mom, my dad, my family
I pray there all they be
And there my grandmas and my grandpas
But how can all this be?

For the last that I did see them
There were much older then than me
But now they're up in Heaven
The same age we seem to be.

Our God will tell to us great stories
Of Jesus Christ His son
How through his blood and suffering
The victory for all of us he won.

Our God will bid us move along
And we will hear our Father say
I love you all My children
Now run along and play.

Happy Birthday Jesus

T'was the night we call Christmas
When here upon earth
A Virgin called Mary
To our Savior gave birth.

He was born in a manger
His bed made of hay
A great shining star
Shone on the place where he lay.

The Angel's told shepherds
Of this new baby boy
They came there to worship
For he filled them with joy.

Three wise men they followed
The star from above
And set there their gifts
And worshiped in love.

On this cold winter night
Father sent us the One
To give us great light
Lord Jesus His Son.

So let us exclaim
To our Father above
With the birth of our Savior
You've shown us Your love.

With all of this said
As we go off to bed
Merry Christmas to All
Through Jesus Christ are we led.

A Letter To Mary

Hello Mary, you don't know me
But I know your Holy name
How an Angel came before you
And did call your Holy name.

To give a message from the Father
You are the Blessed chosen one
To receive and then to carry
Jesus Christ the Father's Son.

When the test was put to Joseph
How He heard the Angel say
The child is of our Father
So wed thee then to Mary, for it is to be God's
way.

Our God the Holy Father
To Bethlehem, He led you there
He placed a star above You
So all would know his Son was there.

You there became the mother
Of Jesus Christ, God's only Son
You're a mother like no other
Our Savior's life was there begun.

Through our Heavenly dear Father
We bless your Holy name
With the birth of our dear Savior
The world will never be the same.

As the Mother, of our Savior
From our Father up above
Makes the day we all call Christmas
A Holy Day that's filled with love.

So a very Merry Christmas
To each and every one
For from Lord our God the Father
Came to us Jesus Christ His Holy Son.

So thank you sweet, sweet Mary
That our Father did favor you
With the birth of Christ our Savior
We can become brand new.

Humility

Humility, Humility
What an easy word to say
Through Jesus Christ our Savior
His humility shows to us, His way.

As you wake up every morning
God's great love for you within
Upon your knees show honor
Humble all yourself to Him.

Then through your day with others
And one may vex you on your way
Be humble and forgiving
A prayer for him do say.

Be ever oh so careful
Of a thing within called pride
Within your flesh it tries so hard
To put humility on the side.

Our pride will only lead us
To a path that's very wide
It reaches down within our souls
Our humility there to hide.

When pride does rule upon our lives
It becomes a raging sin
For then we live to praise ourselves
When all our praise belongs to Him.

So every day upon your knees
To the Lord our God do pray
Please Lord do keep me humble
That I may follow in Christ's way.

Take pleasure in your weakness
In Christ He'll make you strong
It humbles us our weakness
In Jesus Christ we now belong.

When the Lord our God removes from us
Our pride which is our sin
We then can die unto ourselves
So God can wholly move within.

When you know that you are nothing
And Lord God is all in all
It's then God will exalt you
For you harkened to His call.

When humbled then to God and man
And empty there inside
Our Holy God then lives in you
Leaving pride no place to hide.

Our Dearest Friend

God created in His image
A life that is in you and me
A special person that is you
A special person that is me.

He molded oh so carefully
Our lives he had in mind
For every life be different
And all a special kind.

With this life God gave to us
In this life what should we do
Should we only care then for ourselves
Or should we love and care for you.

Our lives through love is meant to share
With all our fellow man
To help the needy and the poor
In every way we can.

It is good to love your neighbor
To your foe love him the same
Be loving and forgiving
Do it all in Jesus' name.

When Christ sat on that mountain side
And the sermon He did give
His words were meant for all of us
His guide how we should live.

And there within God's Holy Book
His Holy words for us to see
He speaks there in to all of us
Of a better life from Him to be.

This special creature God made of us
With a special plan for us to be
Lord Jesus Christ did spill his blood
From sin to set us free.

Let God then make the person
The one He wants for us to be
The plan He made before our birth
With great love for you and me.

Pray to God the Father
Through Jesus Christ his Son
Worthy is the Lord our God
For He is the true and Holy One.

In fellowship do praise his Holy name
All your love to Him do send
For the Lord our God in heaven
Wants to be our dearest friend.

Teach And Serve

Lord God Almighty Father
Sent Jesus Christ His only son
Humbly He came to serve
Our Savior Christ, God's chosen one.

Christ with great humility
Does show how we should live
Our fellow man for us to serve
Our love to them we give.

A humble life did Jesus live
Loving Grace He freely gives
His loving arms He opens them
To believe and come to Him.

Humbled unto God and man
In God's love He has a plan
He lived a life that had no sin
He teaches us to be like Him.

His precious blood upon the cross
To wash away our sins
We died to sin upon His cross
Now Jesus Christ He lives within.

Praise God our Holy Father
Praise Jesus Christ His only son
Spirit lead us in this Trinity
Our new born life through Christ He won.

In Christ My Love

Oh Holy Lord, oh Jesus Christ
It is of You, that is our Light
Your loving heart, such tenderness
Your gracious love, does give us rest.

Your loving arms, You open wide
When trouble comes, we hide inside
You hold us up, and wipe our tears
Your awesome love, relieves our fears.

Oh what a joy, to know the One
My Savior Christ, who is God's Son
Upon the cross, is where He died
God raised Him up, unto His side.

Oh Jesus Christ, He lives again
He comes to us, and lives within
Through Christ His blood, and suffering
He washes us, of all our sin.

Through Jesus Christ, I humbly kneel
To serve my God, and fellow man
Your will my God, do show to me
It is Your love, that set me free.

I pray in Christ, I may be found
When here on earth, that trumpet sounds
Dear Lord my God, to you I pray
In Christ I'll be, on judgment day.

Rolled Away

Jesus Christ His life He give
And He did so we may live
When they led Him with His cross to Calvary.

They raised Him on that cross
For they thought that He had lost
But Twas on that hill
My Savior died for me.

In the tomb where Jesus lay
All our sins for Him to pay
A giant stone was rolled
To close my Savior in.

Three days within He lay
For our sins He there did pay
When God's mighty hand
He rolled that stone away.

He rolled away, He rolled away
With His might hand
God rolled that stone away.

God spoke to Him inside
And said my son arise
For today's the day
That stone is rolled away.

God called Him, come outside
Son You'll soon be at my side
Resurrected!
For ever you will live.

Now with Christ at God's right hand
The Holy Spirit is in man
Thank you Lord my God
Who rolled that stone away.

He rolled away, He rolled away
With the Father's love
He rolled that stone away.

God praise Your Holy Name
The world will never be the same
With Your loving hand
You rolled that stone away.

Jesus died upon that Cross
But there he was not lost
For belief in Him
God rolls our sins away.

Confess of all your sins
And you'll die to live again
Through Jesus Christ our Lord
God rolls our sins away.

Look Up

Look up, unto the heavens
To our Father up above
Look up, to our Lord Jesus Christ
Whom our Father sent with love.

Look up, To God's great chosen one
His own begotten son
With humbleness He came to serve
Our Father's only Son.

Look up, to Him upon that cross
Jesus Christ his blood did spill
With nails they did pierce His skin
For It was the Father's will.

Look up, To our Lord Jesus Christ
New life the Father give
Trust in Him, believe in Him
And there be born again.

Look up, To keep your eyes on Christ
Let Him lead you from within
Let His Holiness consume your soul
That you may live to love like Him.

Look up, to Christ our Savior
Through Him and Him alone
Jesus Christ the only way
To the Father on His throne.

Look up, unto Jesus Christ
As He sets at God's right hand
Look up, for Christ He lives again
And for us He lives within.

Lord God My Everything

How big are you oh Lord my God,
How little here am I?
I often set and wonder
As I gaze up in the sky.

How amazing is the sky so blue
As I set and think of you
For every day you give me Lord
It's a day that is brand new.

Are you in that cloud up there
Or the one that's over there?
The Lord my God's in both of them
My God is everywhere.

The works of you Almighty God
Some things we cannot see
The things we see we know not how
All these wondrous things can be.

Lord my life belongs to You
To sin I died upon Christ's cross
And now with new born life
In Christ I live to You.

Thank you Oh Lord my God
All the things for me You do
I thank You Lord to the end of time
Just to show my love for You.

All that is this universe
Everything God comes from You
From the biggest to the smallest
Oh God it all belongs to You.

You keep in perfect order
All the wondrous things You do
Through each and every second
With great love that comes from You.

Without you Lord
No air to breathe, no beating of my heart
But Oh so many blessings
Came from the very start.

The hair once red upon my head
Now grey it has become
I thank You God for all those years
All my blessings from You have come.

When it be Your will Lord my God
My life on earth is through
I pray dear God You take my soul
To be eternally there with You.

God First

As I wake up every morning
A fresh day that is all new
The first thing that I think of
God I will start my day with You.

With the Spirit here within me
In Your word I start my day
Give me knowledge and great wisdom
That will lead me in Christ's way.

Let my heart be oh so tender
Let my words be sweet and true
Let the Spirit that's within me
Show the love that comes from You.

And as my day does move along
In Your word do keep me strong
In loving and forgiving
Lord keep me from all wrong.

Let me be a blessing
To all my fellow man
Let me help them in their needs
In every way I can.

As this day You gave to me
Let me close it in Your word
I pray dear Lord if the morning comes
We will do it all again.

Always There

As I reach out with my fingers
And stretch them out to touch the air
The air I cannot feel
But Father God I now You're there.

With every beat within my heart
I know they all do come from You
You were there before my start
With a plan that is all new.

Though I be unable
To see the Glory of Your face
With the tenderness You placed in me
You rule my life with all Your Grace.

Through Your Son Lord Jesus Christ
With His blood my sins washed clean
He came here then to live in me
And I, to live through Him.

The truth that is in all Your words
Your truth has set me free
From my mouth the words I say
I pray come from You and not from me.

Through you sweet Lord Jesus
I praise the Father's Holy name
Within Your arms Lord Jesus
You have released me from all shame.

On my knees I worship You
Your name the highest of the high
Dear Lord my God do hold me up
For God in You I'll never die.

Cleansing Blood

What a Great Arising
Has come upon my soul
My Savior Christ forgave me
Without the need of gold.

The silver in this world
It has no hold on me
For the only thing that's precious
Is His blood that cleanses me.

The awesome love of Jesus
Is here within my heart
Since my life I give to Jesus
We never more will part.

The Holy Word in Jesus
God sent the Word for me
To give His live upon the cross
Christ gave his life for me.

Through the Holy Blood of Jesus
His blood it cleanses me
The sweet, sweet name of Jesus
The Word came to set me free.

So Thank You Sweet Lord Jesus
Your life to rescue me
With the blood You spilled upon that cross
That precious blood it cleanses me.

Within Your Arms Lord Jesus
May You ever hold me there
For in Your Arms Lords Jesus
There I live without despair.

I love you sweet, sweet Jesus
Through Your light I now can see
Your blood You spilled upon that cross
That blood is cleanses me.

Temptation

As you move along from day-to-day
With the Love of Christ within
As you try to live a way
A life that's free of sin.

But there from out of nowhere
In Your flesh this thing moves in
It's an ugly thing, temptation
That wants to lead you onto sin.

It tugs and pulls and twists you
Tries it's best to fill your mind
This ugly thing, temptation
As t sneaks up from behind.

You try your best to fight it
Doing all the best you can
This ugly thing, temptation
Sometimes gets the upper hand.

You know the day will come
Temptation comes again
You'll fight it off with all your might
But you see temptation win.

Don't ever get discouraged
And think you just can't win
Go to our Lord Jesus
Who will keep you from all sin.

When temptation comes upon you
Jesus Christ can lead your way
That ugly thing, temptation
Will not win here on this day

Upon your knees to Father God
Give temptation when it comes
He will fight this fight
And sin he'll keep you from.

We try to fight temptation
With our flesh how weak we be
Make God your only all-in-all
From temptation then be free.

Open Up Your Door

Are you in a place in life
You don't really want to be
Are you locked behind a door
That just won't set you free.

Are there things behind that door
Are they sins and wrongs you did
Are they kept behind that door
For there you think they're hid.

Has the burden there behind that door
Ruled your life from day-to-day
Do you hope for there to be a way
To wash those sins away?

There is a way to do it
There is a man that holds the key
To open up and cleanse the sins
That has kept you locked within.

The sins locked behind that door
Ask Jesus to forgive
Jesus will unlock that door
And wash all sins within.

Behind that door that Jesus cleaned
And washed away the sins
He will take the key and lock that door
That you need never go in again.

And if a sin you do commit
The sin please hide no more
Ask Jesus Christ to forgive
And to Heaven open up your door.

He Comforts Me

When trials are before me
And my way I cannot see
In Jesus arms he holds me
With His love He comforts me.

When my heart is filled with sorrow
And my soul does trouble me
With a burden on my shoulders
My Lord Jesus comforts me.

He relieves me of my sorrow
With His Love He touches me
From the things that once were sorrow
Jesus Christ has set me free.

Oh what joy there is in Jesus
To my joy He lives in me
I worship you Lord Jesus
Your great Love You give to me.

The things that stand before me
No matter what they be
All my trust I give you Jesus
For you died to rescue me.

Your Plan

When Father God created you
He had certain things in mind
With all His Love He made of you
A very special kind.

He put there deep within you
His Love how great a gift
Great tenderness within your heart
To give your soul a lift.

And if somehow you've gone astray
Your way you can't find back
Fix your eyes on our Lord Jesus
And those stripes upon his back.

For us Christ took those stripes
Gave his blood upon that Cross
A ransom He there did pay
So we would not be lost.

Put your trust in our Lord Jesus
Walk His path with Christ each day
Keep your eyes upon His actions
On your knees to Him do pray.

Now your back again with Jesus
And God's plan He has for you
Just over that horizon
Where the skies are bright and blue.

Just over that horizon
It's not that far away
It's only just a little hill
If you follow in Christ's way.

Obey His Word and do His will
That you may understand
Jesus stands before you
With God's plan there in His hand.

Go There Every Day

Here's a little thought
That may help you start your day
On your knees to pray to Jesus
Have you been there yet today.

Do you read the words of Jesus
His Love for you is strong
If you spend your day with Jesus
He will keep you from all wrong

In His words there is great wisdom
It is His word that shows the way
Be humble unto Jesus
Put your trust in Him today.

Give thanks to our Lord Jesus
Who gave His Life upon the Cross
His stripes, his blood and suffering
So we would not be lost.

Now then every morning
Before your feet do reach the floor
Pray on your knees to Jesus
That he may open Heaven's door.

Little Bits Of Heaven

There are little bits of Heaven
Our Father sends to us each day
They're little things called children
So very precious in their way.

From the time of their conception
To the moment of their birth
They are from God our Father
Who sent them here to earth.

With great joy these tiny babies
God lays them in our arms
His wondrous love that's in us
To protect them from all harm.

Those tiny little faces
Those tiny little cries
You know the Love of God
Lay right before your eyes.

We know these little children
Rely on us each day
They look to us for guidance
And to love them everyday.

With love do keep your children
And raise them in God's Word
Teach them of Lord Jesus
For he is the Father's Word.

Look upon our children
There's great lessons there within
Jesus said to be with Him
We must first be just like them.

Little children in us they trust
The lessons there to see
For as our children trust in us
Our trust in God must be.

We are of God our Father
Through Jesus Christ the Chosen One
We are His little children
As is, Jesus Christ His Son.

We must be as the little child
Seek the Father through His Son
In Father God we're not alone
But someday at His throne.

Trials

As we live our days upon this earth
There are trials that come our way
Sometimes they seem enormous
And you feel they're here to stay.

They may be trials of anger
They may be trials of fears
They may be trials of things we need
And they bring us then to tears.

As you look upon your trials
As you run them through your mind
These trials that are upon you
You want to leave behind.

Within your mind you do your best
To think these trials away
But then you think they're growing
And you know they're here to stay.

Now step back for a moment
See these trials a different way
They're trials not meant to punish
But to lead you to God's way.

You see that you're not able
To solve these trials on your own
So give your trials to Jesus
As he sets upon His throne.

When trials come upon you
And you cannot understand
Just raise your eyes and look above
There's Jesus, reaching out His helping hand.

Trials are brought before you
Not to cause you any pain
But show to you there is a way
And Lord Jesus is His name

For every trial that comes along
Let your faith in God then grow
Make Father God your all-in-all
His great Love for you He'll show.

Know that it is Father God
Who created everything
So in your trials have faith in Him
And He'll be your everything.

Take your trials and call on God
Put your faith all in His hands
It is then through God's great Grace
Those trials no longer stand.

A Closing Thought

May God cast special Blessings upon you. I
hope you have enjoyed these poems, as much as
I have enjoyed the Spirit working through me
and guiding me.

Acknowledgements

A special thanks to my daughter, Jean Kuhn, through her loving work made publishing this book possible.

A special thanks to my spiritual family, Faith Church, Dyer, Indiana campus.

God Bless,

Gerald M. Allen

Made in the USA
Charleston, SC
07 July 2014